DOOMED HISTORY

MILLIONS DEAD!

The Great Influenza Pandemic, 1918–1920

by Tim Cooke

BEARPORT
PUBLISHING

Minneapolis, Minnesota

Credits: Front Cover, ©Rawpixel.com/Shutterstock; 1, ©Library of Congress; 4–5, ©Everett Historical/Shutterstock; 5, ©Tzido Sun/Shutterstock; 6, ©Everett Historical/Shutterstock; 7t, ©Everett Historical/Shutterstock; 7b, ©arogant/Shutterstock; 8, ©Otis Historical Archives, National Museum of Health and Medicine/Public Domain; 9t, ©Everett Historical/Shutterstock; 9b, ©Museu Nacional d/Art de Catalunya/Kaulak; 10t, ©Imperial War Museum; 10b, ©Cyberbobra/Public Domain; 11, ©Everett Historical/Shutterstock; 12, ©Library of Congress; 13, ©Library of Congress; 14t, ©bmszealand/Shutterstock; 14b, ©Oakland History Room, Oakland Public Library/Public Domain; 15, ©Everett Historical/ Shutterstock; 16, ©WikiMedia Commons/Public Domain; 17t, ©L'Illustration, 4215, 1923/ Public Domain; 17b, ©Everett Historical/Shutterstock; 18, ©U.S. Public Health Service/ Public Domain; 19, ©U.S. Public Health Service/Public Domain; 20, ©Noah Friedlander/ Public Domain; 21, ©Walter Holt Rose/Public Domain; 22, ©Everett Historical/ Shutterstock; 23, ©National Gallery of Norway/National Museum of Art and Design/Public Domain; 24, ©Imperial War Museum; 25, ©courtesy of the Center for American History, the University of Texas at Austin/Robert Runyon Photograph Collection/Public Domain; 26, ©Lev Radin/Shutterstock; 27, ©Library Company of Philadelphia/Public Domain; 28, ©Otis Historical Archives, National Museum of Health and Medicine/Public Domain; 29, ©Y Production/Shutterstock.

Bearport Publishing Company Product Development Team
President: Jen Jenson; Director of Product Development: Spencer Brinker; Senior Editor: Allison Juda; Editor: Charly Haley; Associate Editor: Naomi Reich; Senior Designer: Colin O'Dea; Associate Designer: Elena Klinkner; Associate Designer: Kayla Eggert; Product Development Assistant: Anita Stasson

Brown Bear Books
Children's Publisher: Anne O'Daly; Design Manager: Keith Davis; Picture Manager: Sophie Mortimer

Library of Congress Cataloging-in-Publication Data

Names: Cooke, Tim, 1961- author.
Title: Millions dead! : the great Influenza Pandemic, 1918-1920 / by Tim Cooke.
Other titles: Great influenza pandemic, 1918-1920
Description: Minneapolis, Minnesota : Bearport Publishing Company, [2023] | Series: Doomed history | Includes bibliographical references and index.
Identifiers: LCCN 2022048093 (print) | LCCN 2022048094 (ebook) | ISBN 9798885093972 (library binding) | ISBN 9798885095198 (paperback) | ISBN 9798885096348 (ebook)
Subjects: LCSH: Influenza Epidemic, 1918-1919--Juvenile literature.
Classification: LCC RC150.4 .C66 2023 (print) | LCC RC150.4 (ebook) | DDC 614.5/1809041--dc23/eng/20221007
LC record available at https://lccn.loc.gov/2022048093
LC ebook record available at https://lccn.loc.gov/2022048094

© 2023 Brown Bear Books

This edition is published by arrangement with Brown Bear Books.

For more information, write to Bearport Publishing, 5357 Penn Avenue South, Minneapolis, MN 55419.

CONTENTS

DEVASTATING DISEASE

As World War I (1914—1918) neared its end, a deadly flu **virus** emerged that would kill as many as 100 million people in just 3 years.

A deadly flu, or **influenza**, virus spread as troops moved around during the first world war. It became a devastating **pandemic** that would kill more soldiers than the number that had died in combat. The death rates were so high because health services were limited, and there was no **vaccine**.

Troops returning from World War I spread the deadly flu virus around the world.

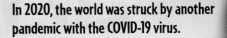

In 2020, the world was struck by another pandemic with the COVID-19 virus.

High Death Rate

The 1918 pandemic affected mainly younger adults, a different population than is usually struck down by the flu. The virus was very **contagious,** making more than 500 million people—almost one-third of the world's population—sick! At the time, public health advice was disorganized and inconsistent, so people did not know how to avoid **infection**.

THE FIRST SIGNS OF TROUBLE

World War I was slowly coming to an end when the virus appeared. At first, everyone thought it was a typical winter flu. But it turned out that this was no ordinary disease.

World War I had started in Europe in 1914. The United States joined the fighting in April 1917, after Germany began attacking U.S. ships. President Woodrow Wilson sent 378,000 troops to Europe, where they joined France and England in the fight against Germany and its allies.

German submarines sank cargo and passenger ships in the Atlantic Ocean.

While they trained, U.S. soldiers lived in camps with between 25,000 and 55,000 men.

Joining the Fight

By June 1917, the United States had introduced a **draft** to increase the size of its army. The new **recruits** trained at large camps and lived in cramped quarters as they got ready to sail to Europe to join the war. Meanwhile, in Europe, millions of people who had been living with war-triggered food shortages were weak and exhausted.

WHAT'S A PANDEMIC?

A widespread outbreak of disease that affects a single area is known as an epidemic. When the outbreak affects many areas or the whole world, it is known as a pandemic. The flu of 1918 was a pandemic, as was the COVID-19 outbreak of 2020.

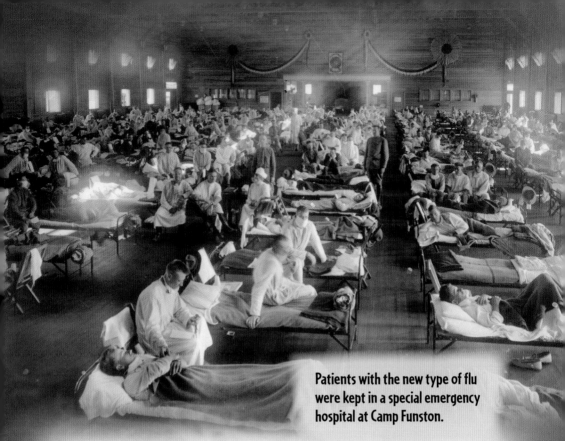

Patients with the new type of flu were kept in a special emergency hospital at Camp Funston.

First Cases

Camp Funston was an army training camp in Fort Riley, Kansas. It could house about 50,000 recruits who lived crowded together in shared spaces. In March 1918, more than 100 soldiers at the fort suddenly became sick with a flu-like disease. Within a week, the number of new cases at the camp had increased five times. Still, doctors thought the sick men had a bad case of ordinary flu.

Field hospitals, like this one in France, were soon filled with flu victims.

Flu Spreads

Reports soon revealed other outbreaks of flu in Kansas, including 18 severe cases and 3 deaths. In Europe, the disease first appeared at a field hospital in France. Throughout the following months, flu spread across the United States, Europe, and Asia. Because the death rate was quite low, however, no one paid much attention.

A NAME FROM SPAIN

The pandemic of 1918 did not start in Spain, but it was first reported in the news when Spanish newspapers described King Alfonso XIII's illness. This is why this pandemic is sometimes called the Spanish flu.

U.S. troops marched in London, England, before sailing to the battlefields in France.

Off to War!

By May 1918, hundreds of thousands of U.S. soldiers had sailed across the Atlantic Ocean. Many of these soldiers were carrying the flu virus, but they didn't know it. In the months that followed, more than 4 million U.S. soldiers would travel to Europe and join the final push to defeat Germany. This movement of so many people helped the disease quickly spread worldwide.

INFLUENZA

Influenza is a highly contagious virus that attacks a person's **respiratory system**. It is spread by tiny droplets pushed into the air when a person coughs or sneezes. The droplets can then easily be breathed in by anyone else standing nearby.

The First Wave

In the first wave of the Great Influenza Pandemic, most of the people infected with the virus were only mildly sick. Their **symptoms** included fever, chills, and low energy. But they usually felt better after a few days. Nobody knew at the time that this disease would soon change into a far more deadly form.

Flu patients filled a U.S. Army hospital in France at the end of World War I.

DISASTER STRIKES

Although the flu raced around the globe, by the summer of 1918, the number of cases fell. The disease seemed to have disappeared.

But soon, a second, deadlier wave of influenza started. Doctors at Camp Devens, an army base in Boston, reported that soldiers were again being struck down by a flu. This time, though, the symptoms were much more serious. By the end of September 1918, the flu had infected a quarter of the entire camp and left 757 dead.

U.S. Army doctors struggled to care for all the victims of the disease.

The Flu Spreads

The new strain of the disease spread rapidly, but people still thought it was a normal winter flu. In Philadelphia, people gathered at a big parade to raise money for the war. The city's public health director said the danger of catching the disease was low. He was wrong. Over the next 10 days, more than 200,000 Philadelphians got sick and about 1,000 died. The city's hospitals and **morgues** were suddenly overflowing.

The parade in Philadelphia was part of a huge effort to raise money for the war.

THAT LIBERTY SHALL NOT PERISH FROM THE EARTH BUY LIBERTY BONDS
FOURTH   LIBERTY   LOAN

A graveyard in Svalbard, Norway, for miners who died in the pandemic

The Pandemic Grows

Between September and November 1918, the second wave of the disease claimed millions of lives, often killing within hours of infection. A victim who felt fine at breakfast might be dead by dinner. The disease hit people between the ages of 20 and 40 the hardest. When they got sick, their skin turned blue and their lungs filled with fluid. Many **suffocated** to death.

TEMPORARY HOSPITALS

Schools, homes, and public buildings soon had to be converted into temporary hospitals. So many doctors got sick from the disease that these places were run by medical students, some of whom had not even finished their training.

Shortage of Medics

The United States and other countries were not ready for the speed at which the pandemic hit. Hundreds of thousands died because they could not get medical help. With proper care, it was often possible to survive the flu. Because of the war, however, there was a severe shortage of doctors and nurses in hospitals.

The number of doctors and nurses serving in the army caused a shortage of caregivers at non-military hospitals.

War Ends

On November 11, 1918, Germany surrendered, and World War I was officially over. Hundreds of thousands of people gathered around the world to celebrate the end of the world's bloodiest conflict, and millions of soldiers left camps and battlefields to go home. As they traveled around the world on crowded ships and trains, they helped rapidly spread the flu virus.

New Yorkers gathered in Manhattan to celebrate the end of World War I.

Coming Home

In all, 40 percent of sailors in the U.S. Navy and 36 percent of soldiers in the U.S. Army became infected with the virus. Many soldiers brought the deadly disease home to their families. People still did not understand how easily this flu could be passed from person to person.

ASPIRIN POISONING

With no cure for the flu and so many young people dying suddenly, the United States Surgeon General said taking aspirin could help. But the recommended dose was so high that some people died from aspirin poisoning.

Bayer-Tablets and Capsules of Aspirin

Made on the Banks of the Hudson River

For Your Protection

Public Health

In order to slow the flu's spread, public health officials began offering advice on how to prevent infection. But they did not all make the same recommendations. Some medical experts told people to wash their hands and use disinfectant. Others advised people to limit contact with other people or wear masks to protect themselves. The public was confused by these different suggestions.

Posters gave the public advice about how to avoid infection.

Coughs and Sneezes Spread Diseases

As Dangerous as Poison Gas Shell:

SPREAD OF SPANISH INFLUENZA MENACES OUR WAR PRODUCTION

Police officers in Seattle wore face masks to protect themselves from the flu.

Cities Respond

Although it was becoming clear that the pandemic was very serious, there was still no unified response in the United States. Many cities shut down public buildings, such as churches, libraries, and theaters. Some businesses were forced to close. In San Francisco and Seattle, residents were ordered to wear face masks, while other cities forced people who were sick to go into **quarantine**. Some cities even banned spitting, which was thought to spread the disease.

A THIRD WAVE

By late in the fall of 1918, the second wave of the flu was dying down. Many people assumed the worst was over. They were wrong.

That winter, a third wave emerged. This version of the disease was less deadly but even more contagious. In the first five days of 1919, at least 1,800 new flu cases were reported in San Francisco. People were reluctant to admit there was flu in their home, so many cases went unreported. This only helped to spread the virus further.

More than 100 people died during the third wave of flu that hit San Francisco in January 1919.

Inuit Tragedy

Some communities, including the Inuit settlement at Brevig Mission in Alaska, were completely devastated by the disease. Over just five days, 72 of the 80 adults living in Brevig Mission died after being infected. Because the local Inuit population hadn't experienced any kind of previous flu, the virus was deadly to almost everyone in this group who caught it.

FROZEN IN TIME

The body of a young Inuit woman who died from the flu that ravaged Brevig Mission was buried in frozen ground. There, she remained perfectly preserved. In 1997, scientists analyzed **genetic** material from her remains and discovered that the 1918 flu virus belonged to a type of influenza called H1N1. This type still exists today.

A Traveling Virus

The second and third waves of the flu hit other countries hard, too. The virus usually appeared first near a country's ports as ships arrived from around the world. From there, infected passengers on trains carried the virus from city to city. In early 1919, Australia lifted a ban it had put on foreign ships during the first two years of the pandemic. Soon after, the third wave of the virus arrived in the country, killing 12,000 people. Even remote islands in the Pacific Ocean recorded deaths from the flu.

U.S. soldiers gargled with disinfectant to try to protect themselves from the disease.

The Norwegian artist Edvard Munch painted himself as he recovered from influenza.

Devastation

In London, England, so many police officers were sick with the flu that they could not keep the city safe. There was a report of 61 people collapsing in the city streets over a single 48-hour period. In the United States, 1 out of every 200 infected people died. However, the country most affected by the flu was India, where 6.7 million people died after catching the virus. That was more than 5 percent of India's total population.

A Sick President

The peace settlement that ended World War I was discussed in the Palace of Versailles just outside Paris, France.

In April 1919, the world's leaders gathered in Paris, France, to discuss a settlement to end World War I. Shortly afterward, U.S. president Woodrow Wilson collapsed with the flu. Government officials did not want to alarm Americans, so they reported that the president had caught a cold because of chilly, rainy weather in Paris. Wilson survived the illness.

A HEAVY TOLL

About 20 million people died during World War I, and another 21 million were injured. The **casualties** were higher than any previous war due to the use of deadly new weapons, such as machine guns.

A Fourth Wave

For the rest of 1919 and until the summer of 1920, the number of people getting the flu remained high. This fourth wave of the disease caused spikes in infection rates in different places at different times, but the death rates were much lower. People who caught the virus were sick for a few days but then recovered quickly. By the summer of 1920, the Great Influenza Pandemic was finally reaching its end.

After the pandemic ended, many people wanted to have fun. This included enjoying jazz music, which became very popular in the 1920s.

WHAT HAPPENED NEXT

As infection rates dropped in the 1920s, many people quickly forgot about the devastation caused by the flu.

Throughout the pandemic, the media had not reported on the flu as much as they had the war. After all, people had been used to deaths from diseases such as cholera and diphtheria. In some ways, the 1918 flu was seen as just another deadly disease.

The 1920s, also known as the Roaring Twenties, was a carefree time for many people.

The Roaring Twenties

After the war and pandemic ended, people were relieved and wanted to enjoy themselves. In the 1920s women were gaining more freedoms, and daily life had never been so good for so many people. The future looked promising for many. Sadly, this upbeat mood ended with the **stock market** crash of October 1929, which led to the **Great Depression**. This period of hardship would last for more than a decade.

A LOST GENERATION

Almost 117,000 Americans died fighting in World War I. The Great Flu Pandemic killed another 675,000. This loss of life took a huge toll on the United States.

Public Health System

Before the Great Influenza Pandemic, there was no organized public health system in most countries. By the time the pandemic ended, that had begun to change. Governments started collecting health **data** to identify outbreaks of disease. By 1925, all U.S. states reported diseases to a central office that created a warning system to help spot early signs of a new pandemic.

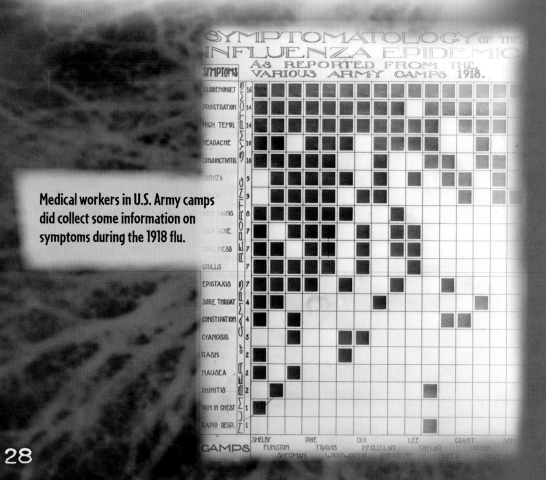

Medical workers in U.S. Army camps did collect some information on symptoms during the 1918 flu.

Advances in medicine have allowed scientists to identify the exact virus that caused the 1918 pandemic.

Decoding the Virus

It took experts a long time to figure out where the 1918 flu virus came from and how it behaved. In recent years, a sample taken from the body of a flu victim showed that the virus had originated in birds and later crossed over to pigs and humans. Learning more about the 1918 virus is helping scientists develop vaccines to fight off future pandemics.

OTHER PANDEMICS

There were flu pandemics in 1957, 1968, and 2009. The 2020 COVID-19 pandemic killed about 1 percent of the global population. But none of these flus was as terrible as the Great Influenza Pandemic of 1918. It is estimated that this virus killed between 50 and 100 million people—anywhere from 3 to 5 percent of the world's population.

KEY DATES

1917

April The United States enters World War I.

1918

March Outbreak of a flu-like sickness is reported at Camp Funston in Kansas.

April More people get sick in Kansas and in France.

May The first wave of the influenza pandemic hits Europe and the United States.

September The second wave hits. Death rates rise across the United States.

October Flu death rates increase around the world.

November 11 World War I officially ends.

December Public health education programs start across the United States.

1919

January The third wave hits.

April President Woodrow Wilson catches the flu in France.

1920

Summer The fourth wave of the virus slows down, and the pandemic finally ends.

1925 U.S. states start to report infectious diseases.

1997 Scientists successfully remove a virus sample from a victim of the 1918 pandemic so they can study it.

QUIZ How much have you learned about the Great Influenza Pandemic? It's time to test your knowledge! Then, check your answers on page 32.

1. **Why was the 1918 pandemic known as the Spanish flu?**
   a) It started in Spain.
   b) A different disease started in Spain at the same time.
   c) Spanish newspapers reported that King Alfonso XIII of Spain caught it.

2. **Who were the most likely people to get sick?**
   a) adults between 20 and 40
   b) children younger than 10
   c) people older than 65

3. **How was the virus spread?**
   a) by touching surfaces
   b) by eating infected food
   c) through droplets in the air

4. **Which country had the highest death rate?**
   a) The United States
   b) India
   c) France

5. **How many Americans were killed by the flu and in the war?**
   a) 50,000 (flu) and 205,000 (war)
   b) 344,000 (flu) and 500,000 (war)
   c) 675,000 (flu) and 117,000 (war)

GLOSSARY

casualties people hurt or killed in a war or disaster

contagious easily spread from person to person

data information, especially in the form of numbers

draft a system of forcing people to join the military

field hospitals temporary hospitals near a battlefield where doctors give emergency care to wounded people

genetic relating to how certain physical characteristics, traits, or tendencies are passed down to children from their parents

Great Depression a period in the 1930s when many people in the United States lost their jobs and were very poor

infection the process of becoming sick with a disease

influenza a disease caused by a virus with symptoms that include fever, coughing, and aches

morgues buildings that store dead bodies before they are buried

pandemic an outbreak of a disease that affects many people around the world at the same time

quarantine a system of keeping sick people apart from others to stop the spread of a disease

recruits people brought into the army to train to become soldiers

respiratory system the system of organs, including the lungs, that helps people breathe and provides oxygen for the body

stock market a place where ownership shares of companies are bought and sold

suffocated died from not being able to breathe

symptoms the things that happen to a body because of an illness

vaccine a medicine that can be given to people to prevent them from catching a particular disease

virus a tiny organism that causes diseases in humans and animals

INDEX

READ MORE

Hamen, Susan E. *The 12 Worst Health Disasters of All Time (All-Time Worst Disasters).* Mankato, MN: 12-Story Library, 2019.

Krasner, Barbara. *Influenza: How the Flu Changed History (Infected!).* North Mankato, MN: Capstone Press, 2019.

Thomas, Rachael L. *Viral Spread: Then and Now (Pandemics).* Minneapolis: Abdo Publishing, 2022.

LEARN MORE ONLINE

1. Go to **www.factsurfer.com** or scan the QR code below.

2. Enter **"Millions Dead"** into the search box.

3. Click on the cover of this book to see a list of websites.

Answers to the quiz on page 30

Answers to the quiz on page 30
1) C; 2) A; 3) C; 4) B; 5) C